First light: the Clun Valley
from Bury Ditches hill fort

Mind where you go

Church Stretton and Caer Caradoc

Townbrook Hollow

The Long Mynd and Stretton Hills

In the Shropshire Hills a single step can take you on a journey of 6,000 miles or 600 million years. Beneath your feet is chaos. Earthquakes, volcanoes, tongues of ice ... for hundreds of millions of years. It was a rocky road before the hills combined beauty with serenity.

Do travellers on road or rail through Church Stretton realise they are following a tear in the Earth's crust? Would they be quite so relaxed if they knew that tectonic plates once made this one of the most active parts of the Earth's surface?

When most of this country was below the sea the Long Mynd was a great island surrounded by beaches. As the tongues of ice came and went they deepened the main valley (along the line of the A49). The 'batches' or hollows like Carding Mill Valley or Ashes Hollow were formed by streams cutting their way down to the new level. Where the streams cross a band of more resistant rock you have today's attractive waterfalls.

The upheavals have produced jaw-dropping panoramas and a treat for golfers – the 14th at Church Stretton at 365m (1,200ft) is one of the highest greens in England. Manicured order from chaos.

From Brown Clee, looking south to Titterstone Clee

Looking back: Brown Clee

We owe one of the best views in England to geology. The dolerite, known locally as dhustone, which caps Titterstone Clee and its neighbour Brown Clee, has protected the summits from erosion.

And so you have the highest 'A' road in the Midlands and the highest summit south of the Pennines. Once it was the highest coal mine. They say to the east you have to travel to the Urals to find its match. From the summit of Titterstone Clee there are 360-degree views.

The Wenlock Era

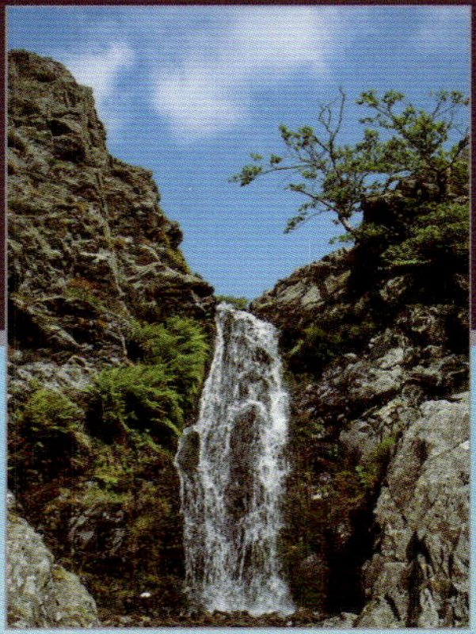

Light Spout waterfall

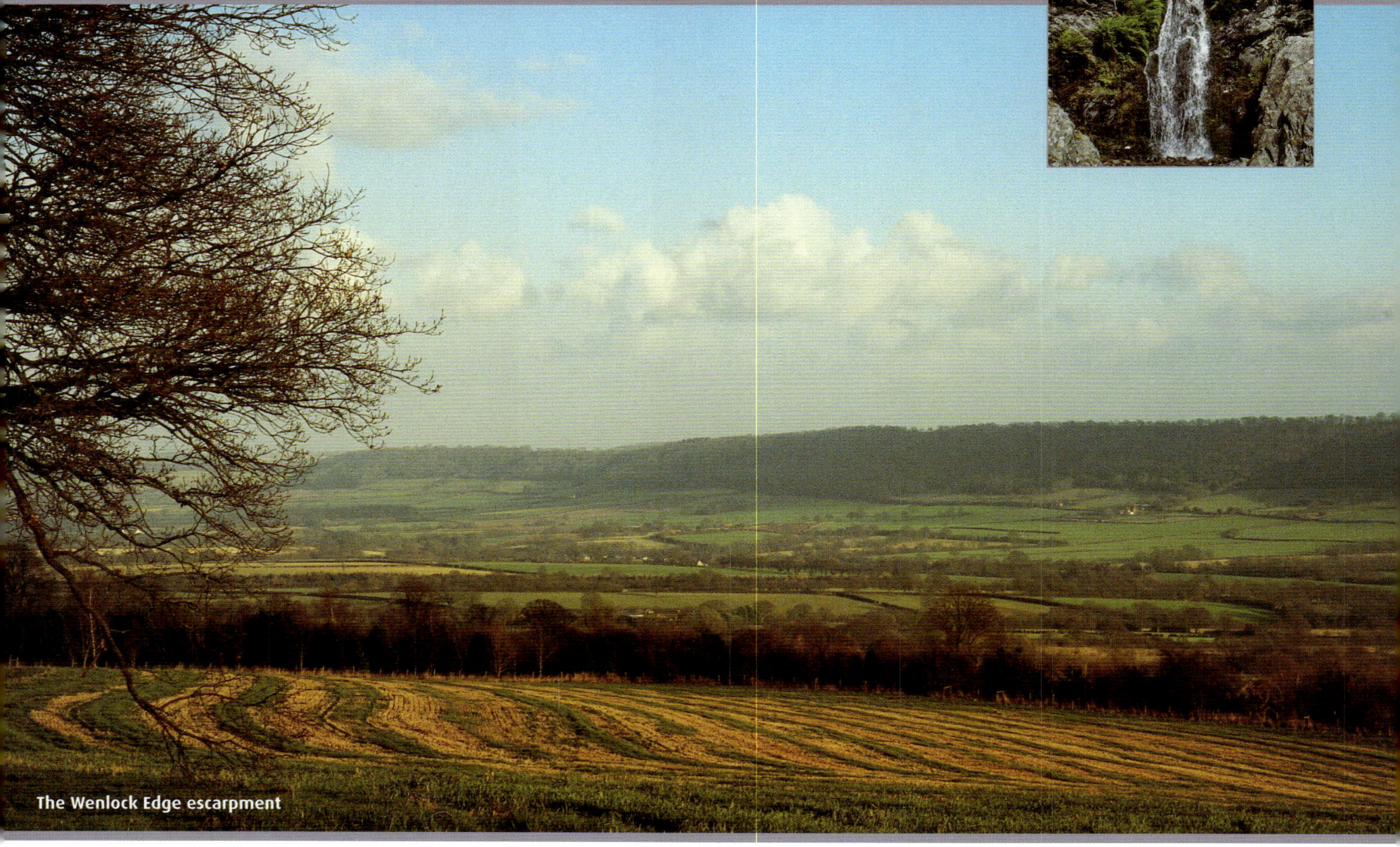

The Wenlock Edge escarpment

All over the world geologists refer to some of their rocks as 'Wenlockian'.

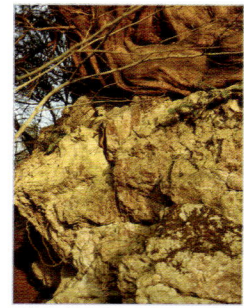

Wenlock Edge limestone

Shropshire had difficulty making up its mind where it wanted to be. For a while we tried south of the Equator with the Seychelles as our neighbours. Sounds fanciful? Take a closer look at Wenlock Edge, the finest geological escarpment in Britain. The fossils which have made this a world-famous site include corals, sea lilies and shells. So here in the middle of Britain is a series of coral reefs 20 miles long which was formed 425 million years ago.

You can still find pieces of coral as you walk along the Edge. Every piece of limestone you pick up seems to contain shellfish which look exactly like shells on the beach today.

Stiperstones tors

The Devil's Chair, Stiperstones

The Stiperstones is one of our wildest places. The fractured white tors of quartzite are stark, even quite hostile. Formed at first from beach sand, the dramatic carving of the rocks was executed during the last ice age.

The Devil believed that if only the Stiperstones could be made to sink into the bowels of the earth, England and all God-fearing people would perish, and so he tried to weigh it down with boulders.

What better setting for the end of the world? The legend of the Seven Whistlers has it that six birds are searching the hillside for a long-lost companion.

When they find him, the world will end.

Bury Ditches

'Good fences make good neighbours' Robert Frost

After millions of years of rock and roll, it was time for mankind.

Early in our existence, long before the leylandii, the search for peace and quiet began. Prehistoric men and women found it on these hilltops. Climb Brown Clee, Bury Ditches, Caer Caradoc, Nordy Bank, The Burrow, The Wrekin, – and pause for breath. Here are small forts and enormous strongholds. This is archaeology with the most spectacular panoramas – commanding the countryside, keeping a weather eye out for strangers.

Mitchell's Fold

Ramparts of Nordy Bank hill fort

Walk around the still massive ramparts and ditches. What must they have been like to withstand years of erosion? The scale of these hill forts is mind-boggling. How did our ancestors create them? Imagine building them with just your family and the neighbours. It could take centuries of gradual development.

Most likely the forts were permanent settlements where the terrain made them easier to defend. In climbing these hills you walk in the footsteps of your ancestors from 3,000 years ago. Look around you; they saw the same sunrises and sunsets. Here they placed their sacred ceremonial sites for burials and stone circles.

Sunrise, The Wrekin

Offa's Dyke …
at its finest and most inspiring

Near Spoad Hill

Offa's Dyke, Llanfair Hill

An early form of national service produced Britain's longest monument. When King Offa ordered 'the construction of a large rampart from sea to sea', it was time to start digging. Men from the border country had to build 4ft of dyke (or send food in lieu). The scene was set for stability and trade.

The Dyke is at its most impressive between Spoad Hill and Llanfair Hill above Clun. How fitting that the Dyke also reaches its highest point here, man in friendly competition with nature to dominate.

This was no Berlin or Hadrian's Wall, relative peace was needed for such a mammoth undertaking. Apart from its defensive role, it marked the frontier and defined the routes across it.

The scene was set for stability and trade.

'lived in by people … beginning to believe in good intentions' Henry James

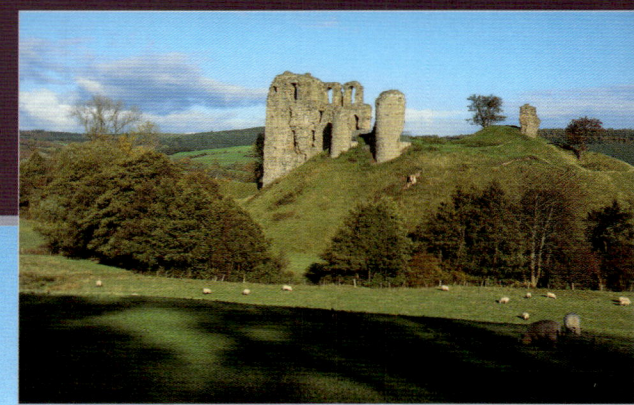

The 13th-century Great Tower, Clun Castle

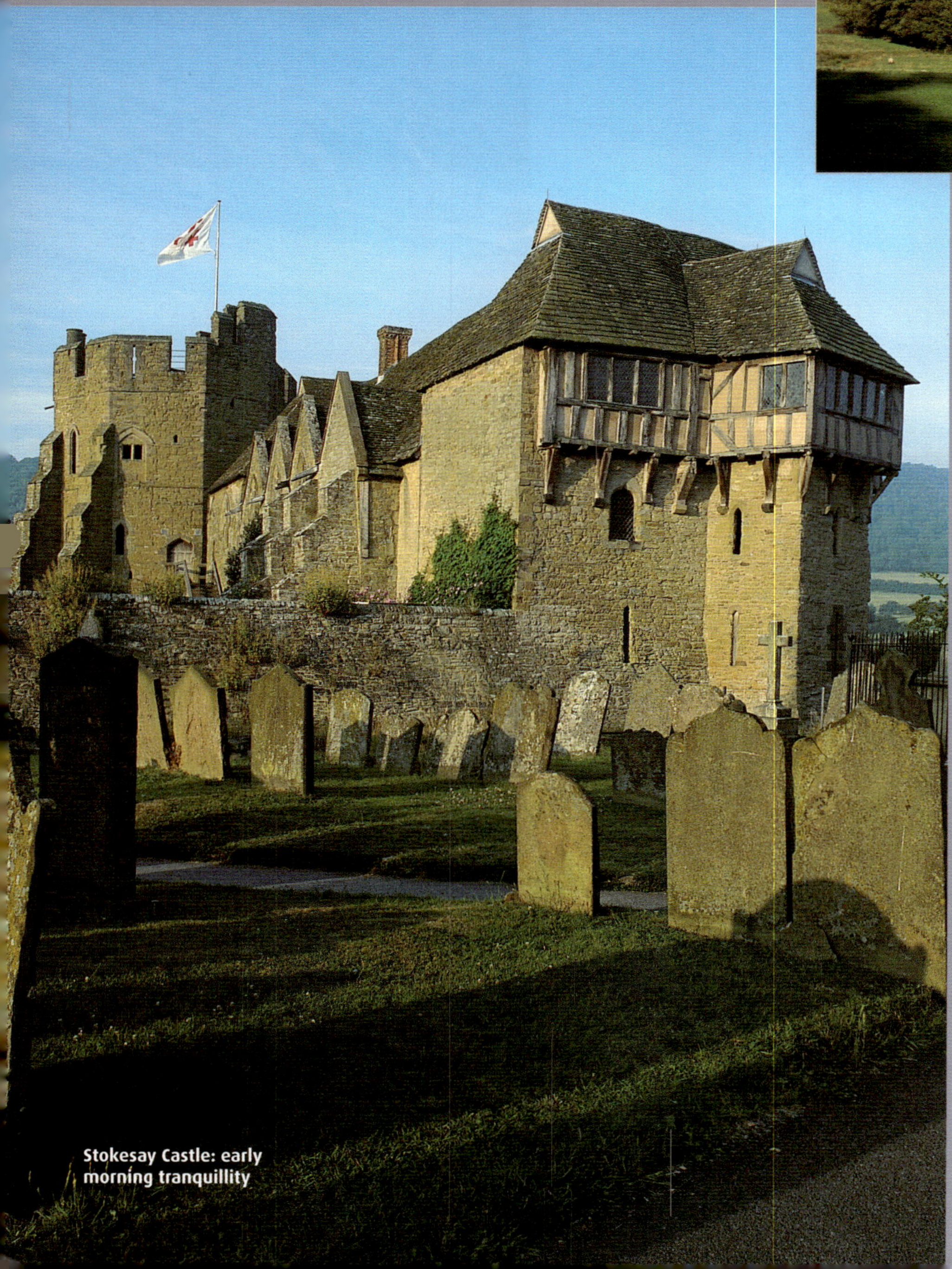

Stokesay Castle: early morning tranquillity

Stokesay Castle is not just the most picturesque of Shropshire's ancient monuments. Without the profits from the wool trade it could not have been built. Wales had been conquered and the risk of invasion had receded. Lawrence of Ludlow, the greatest wool merchant of his day, replaced a grim fortress with this elegant fortified manor house – the finest and best preserved in England. It is more domestic than military.

English Heritage captures the feeling: 'The castle itself nestles in the peaceful countryside.' Over the gatehouse the carved timbers depict Adam and Eve in the Garden of Eden.

Shropshire was turning into a paradise.

Harmony

Early morning on The Lawley

It isn't just time which has created a unique harmony between the hill forts, Offa's Dyke or Stokesay and the landscape of the Shropshire Hills. All were built by people who understood the terrain and the materials. The result is extraordinary – monuments in some of the most prominent places which embellish, not disfigure, them.

Happily, you can explore using roads, tracks and paths, which also have great stories to tell. Lowland Shropshire was densely forested and so tracks took the easier and safer course over high ground. Walking or riding along the Portway on the Long Mynd you are following in the footsteps of Neolithic axe traders. In the Middle Ages it was a King's Highway.

Bromlow Callow

Edenhope Hill, Offa's Dyke

For hundreds of years until the railways, Welsh cowboys, drovers, brought livestock to the markets of Shropshire and beyond. The Kerry Ridgeway is the best known. Hugging the high ground until it drops down to Bishop's Castle it never dips below a thousand feet.

Telltale signs of a drove road are the frequent clumps of pine trees. 'Callow' means a bald hill. How then did Bromlow Callow acquire what the *Independent*'s travel writer described as 'a fetching coronet of trees'? Long before road signs, these pine trees are thought to have been planted by drovers as a landmark that could be seen for miles and made navigation easier.

Moving the mountains

Dereliction, Brown Clee

Rock and rust

Marble quarry, Clee Hill

Our ancestors have carved out their existence here for the last 10,000 years. Sometimes it's just a trace – medieval villages in Corvedale deserted when a mini ice age drove the inhabitants down into the valley. At others, like the Pyramids, it's civil engineering on a huge scale over decades.

Go to Snailbeach, the Clee Hills or Wenlock Edge and you can see where Shropshire's mineral wealth was blasted, quarried, gouged out of the earth. Whole hillsides have been shipped elsewhere – millions of tons of road stone, limestone and lead.

The very street the house stood in might be paved with the hard-wearing dhustone from the Clee Hills.

Titterstone Clee

Titterstone Clee, once bedlam, now silent

Victorian towns and cities would have fallen apart without the mineral wealth of Shropshire. Without the limestone from the quarries and kilns of Wenlock Edge, no iron and steel, no mortar and plaster, poor quality glass and paper, inferior road surfaces and plants that struggle in the field and garden for lack of lime. A 19th-century house without Shropshire's mines and quarries would have been a poor thing.

Disused limestone quarry, Wenlock Edge

*The steam engines, the crushers, the inclined planes,
the railways, are silent.*

Snailbeach

Without the lead mines of Snailbeach no pipes, no paint, no flashings for the roof, no gutters and downpipes and no window frames. The mines, once the richest in Europe, provided the raw material for paint, pipes, pottery glazes and pewter. If all this lead was bad for the health (not to mention the bullets), you could be buried in a vault or coffin lined with lead.

Corndon Hill and Wales, from the Stiperstones

Pennerley – overlooked by the Devil's Chair

Smelthouse chimney, Snailbeach

The poisonous clouds of lead and arsenic, which rumour has it would fell any bird unwise enough to take the direct route, are no more. Peregrine falcons nest where the stone was quarried. The National Nature Reserve overlooks the surprisingly intact buildings of the lead mines. Purple heather has replaced smoke and steam.

With a little help from us, Nature has largely won the battle to reclaim its territory. However, if you want to pay homage to the men and women whose sweat greased the wheels of the Industrial Revolution, look no further than these hills.

'For I am among thee and maketh things grow'

Clun Green Man

The Hollies, Stiperstones

'Great trees border his cloak, their branches interlacing across his chest and, uniquely, his leaf face is crowned with deer antlers.'

Walcot Wood

The Clun Green Man personifies our union with the animal as well as the vegetable world. He represents past centuries of living in harmony with the landscape.

We inherit our trees from our ancestors. Some are the descendants of the first trees to colonise the Shropshire Hills after the last ice age. The earliest example of our union with nature is a 'living giant'. The yew in All Saints churchyard, Norbury is one of the ten largest in Britain, 10m (33ft) in girth. David Bellamy, the botanist, reckons it to be at least 2,700 years old, twice as old as the church. We owe it therefore to pagans. A mile away but nearly 2,500 years its junior is Linley Beeches.

One of the most beautiful sights in Shropshire

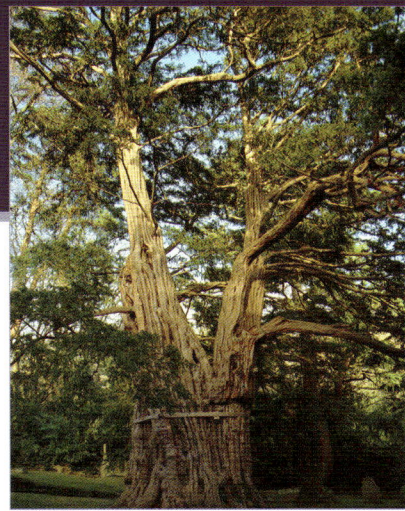

Ancient yew tree, Church Preen

Visible from miles around, this avenue of ancient beeches strides up Linley Hill and follows the ridge. The trees and the landscape are a perfect marriage. There is sadness as well as beauty, as these near 300-year-old trees approach their end. For our great-great-great-great grandchildren the Linley Beeches Support Group are planting replacements.

In a small valley protected from storm and pollution is once-neglected Walcot Wood. The National Trust is preserving nearly 50 veteran oaks. These 400-year-old, unusually shaped trees were into their second century when Clive of India bought the estate. Each tree is managed individually for its unique collection of lichens. The wood is on the Shropshire Way and a visit can be combined with Bury Ditches hill fort.

Brook Vessons, on the northern slopes of the Stiperstones, has a whole cluster of giant trees. You can see six of Britain's broadest mountain ash trees, including the supreme champion. Within just 100m (328 ft) of the rowans are the biggest birch, the biggest holly and the biggest crab apple tree in Shropshire.

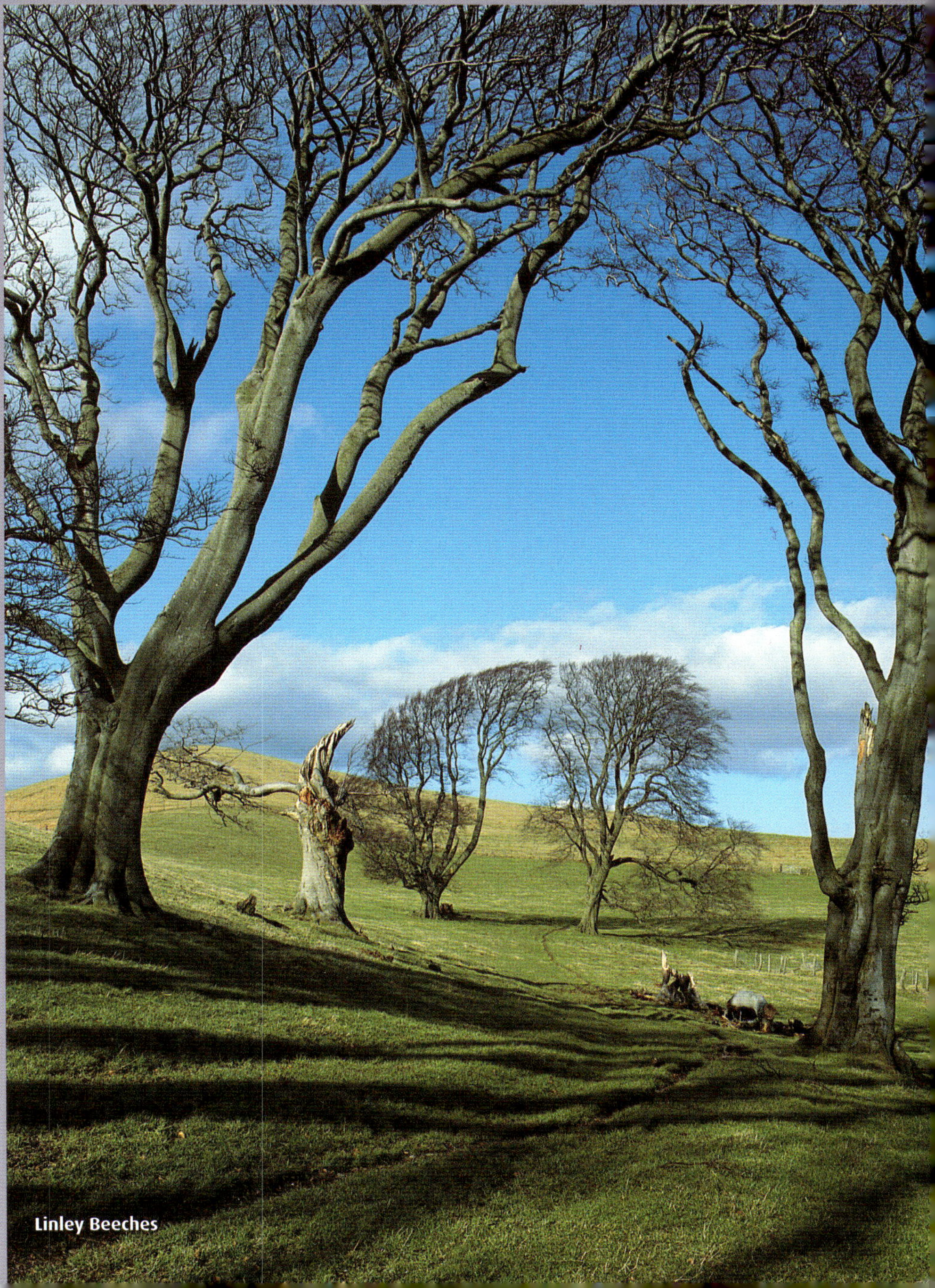

Linley Beeches

In valleys of springs of rivers,
By Ony and Teme and Clun,
The country for easy livers,
The quietest under the sun,

Black poplar

Clunbury and the Clun Valley, from Clunbury Hill

Housman might have added the Corve and the Kemp to his rivers – miles of tree-lined rivers that are one of the most distinctive features of the Shropshire Hills.

The tallest of our native trees, the black poplar thrives on its closeness to these Shropshire streams and rivers. Its dense round crown has been compared to 'a green thunder-cloud'.

When the poplars provided bean poles, fruit baskets, sheep hurdles, matches and even First World War rifle butts there was little need to protect them. Yet it is now one of our most endangered native trees. Even to preserve today's numbers requires between seven and ten trees to be planted for each one to reach maturity. Over 400 black poplars have been planted on over 100 sites.

Enthusiasm and expertise are helping to conserve and enhance the landscape

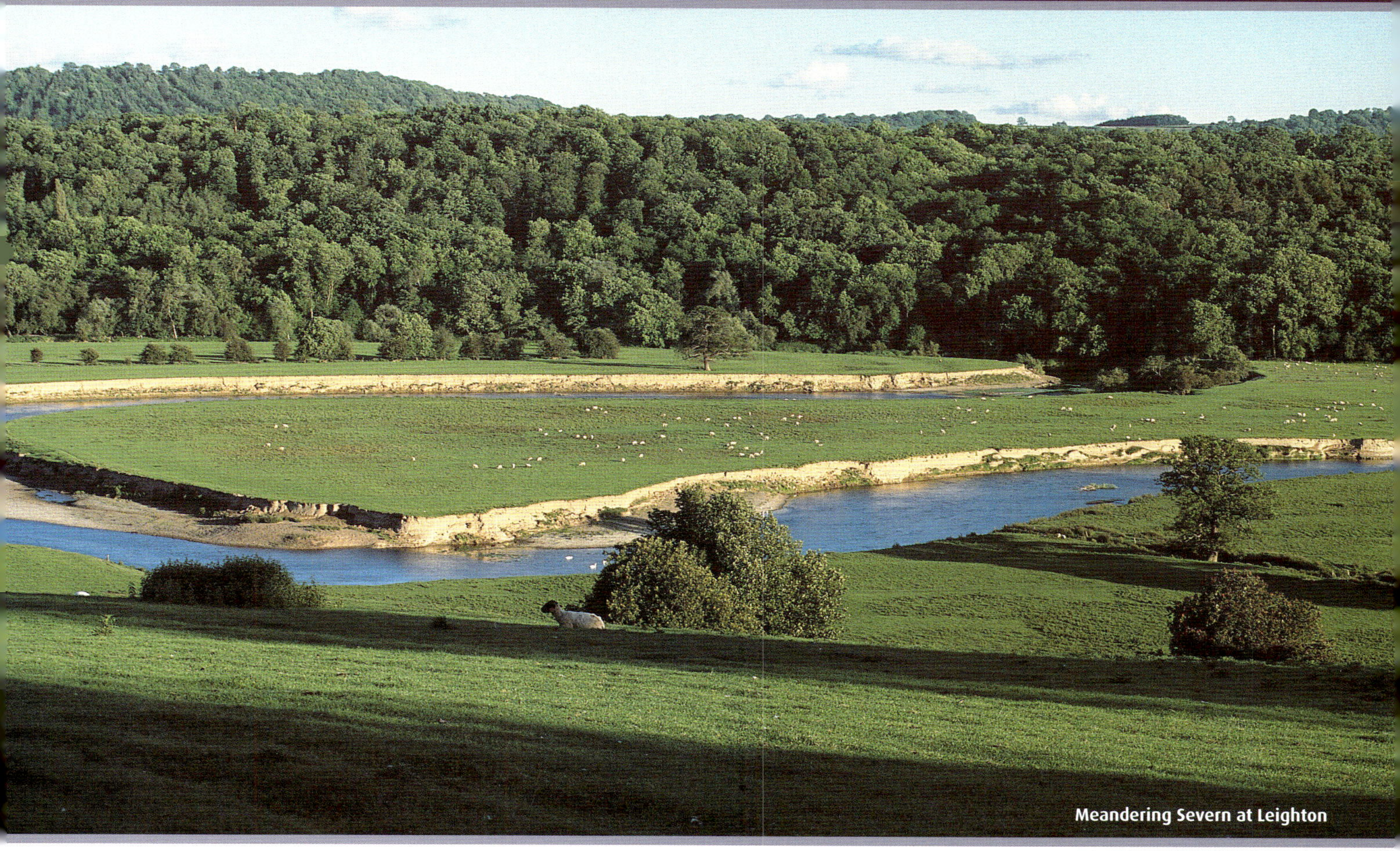

Meandering Severn at Leighton

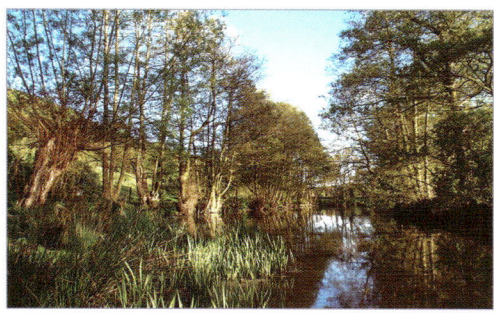

Alders flanking the River Onny

It is easy to take our landscape for granted. River woodlands are valuable wildlife refuges and corridors. Anyone who has walked these river banks will be familiar with the alder, locally known as Waller or Woller. It is the commonest tree in the county outside woodlands and forests. If they are to thrive they must be coppiced even without the traditional market for clog soles and fuel.

For a month or so each summer the colours, sounds and scents of wildflower meadows make them a magical place. Small patches of traditional unimproved hay meadows are being identified and grant-aided to preserve some of the most colourful fields in the county.

'The Hills of Heaven' Mary Webb

Mary Webb was thinking of a gentler part of the Shropshire Hills when she wrote these lines. Yet it is the local dhustone – black basalt – which has inspired internationally renowned sculptor Stephen Cox.

Clee Hill 2004 **dhustone sculpture by Stephen Cox weighs 25 tonnes**

For over 20 years he has scoured the earth for challenging stones. He has carved some of the hardest and most intractable materials ever quarried. Stones whose exceptional hardness has deterred many sculptors.

When he chose to make his home and UK studio on the slopes of Titterstone Clee, he was unaware of its history and geology. Inspired by finding the Clee Hills on *Mappa Mundi*, the 13th-century map of the world in Hereford Cathedral, he was delighted to find dhustone from the local quarry was as hard, dark and exhilarating to work as the Indian basalt he had gone halfway round the world to find.

Primeval outcrops, Stiperstones

Beverley Fry has her studio near Much Wenlock. Her work has been accepted by the Royal Academy, with exhibitions in London, Paris, Dublin and now the US. Initially she explored the fields and meadows around the Wrekin and walked Wild Edric's Way. She has sought inspiration for her painting when cycling, walking and admiring hedgerow flowers. She finds the Stretton Hills are most inspirational in winter.

My subjects are drawn directly from the farm life and the cows I have come to love

Spring Storm oil painting by Beverley Fry

'My subject matter is drawn directly from farm animals, landscape and flowers around me. To walk in the Shropshire Hills is always very healing for my creative practice. Writing with the beauty around me gives me great inner peace and joy. This forms at times a foundation for my work. I prefer to capture something of the essence of the Shropshire landscape rather than just one specific place. It leaves me free to make the more abstract qualities that balance a picture.

'Painting cows is unusual – I am developing the landscape around the relationships that cattle have with each other and the seasons. The cows deserve our respect. They are a brilliant source of inspiration for my new paintings and drawings alongside my more familiar flower images.'

Canoodling Cattle charcoal drawing by Beverley Fry

A grand affair with castellated gutter and some splendid hopper heads embossed with heraldic dogs, by Richard Craven

'All my buildings embody something of my client, the site and me.

Late summer, Long Mynd

The Royal Hennery. This was built for Prince Charles at Highgrove. His 50th birthday present to himself

No one can seek inspiration closer to home than Richard Craven, a woodworker and forester who lives in the Corvedale. His home, Jack Clee's cottage, may have been built as a kind of folly to enhance the view from the great house at Diddlebury. It's on his doorstep, so to speak, that he finds ideas for his timber buildings and follies.

'All my buildings embody something of my client, the site and me. I use a lot of oak and home-grown timber mixed with copper and lead and blacksmith-made fittings .... Any building must be at one with its site.'

The Cabin. Made from oak and brick. The tower holds three bunks and has a proper fireplace

Housman, Mary Webb, Ellis Peters, even DH Lawrence have drawn inspiration from the Shropshire landscape.

Nine writers were commissioned to produce a dramatic monologue – their response to a week in one of the most rural parts of the UK. White Open Spaces is a Pentabus Theatre project with BBC Radio Drama

Mind you, it's pretty.

'That's what I think about the country. It's a place where stuff goes on that you wouldn't want to know about, stuff that's hidden away in all this open space, these fields of earth and dark, dark nights with no sulphur glow and no neighbours around to hear. Mind you, it's pretty.'

Each year the Arvon Foundation attracts nearly a thousand writers to its creative writing centre, The Hurst in the Clun Valley. Creative benches are placed strategically around the 30 acres of woodland, gardens and a lake, opportunity for absorption in and contemplation of the landscape.

Published writers looking for fresh inspiration, beginners and shoolchildren, all are treated as artists in their own right. They draw inspiration from a week's intense experience.

Hills of Home

Sun Inn, Clun

Outgoing tide: Upper Darnford, Long Mynd

The Shropshire Hills are much more than seven ranges with panoramic vistas. Nor are they some vast open-air museum of rural life. They are home to dozens of villages and hamlets. The towns of Bishop's Castle, Church Stretton, Cleobury Mortimer, Clun, Craven Arms, Ludlow and Much Wenlock are centres for markets, shops and festivals.

Almost 80 per cent of the area is devoted to farming. Farming has shaped the landscape – think of those woolly lawnmowers who have kept the place in trim. The hills have their own breeds of sheep, the Clun, the Kerry Hill and the Shropshire. Much of Ludlow's culinary fame rests on the produce of these hills. Visitors can meet producers and their livestock face-to-face by taking a farm tour.

Real ale in Bishop's Castle

Church Stretton Food Festival

A cornucopia of food and drink awaits the visitor. In the 1970s half the brew pubs in England were in Shropshire. The Hills are still Top of the Hops with five micro breweries. These local ales are served at many pubs, along with perfect hand-raised pork pies and traditional breed meat reared not far from the kitchen door.

Near Round Oak, Craven Arms

Oh I have been to Ludlow fair
And left my necktie God knows where,
And carried half-way home, or near,
Pints and quarts of Ludlow beer;

A E Housman

You can't beat shopping in the open air. Graze amongst the market stalls. Hunt down the farm shops, the artisan bakers, the craftsmen cheeses and WI stalls. Look out for whinberries from the Long Mynd or the Stiperstones. Food always tastes better outdoors. Everyone has their own idea of a favourite spot for a picnic. How about the banks of a Corvedale stream or on top of the Wrekin?

Even the quietest places need to go wild occasionally. In Clun three thousand people come to see The Green Man enter accompanied by the May Queen, morris dancers, Jack the Jester on stilts, wandering minstrels, medieval knights, ladies and foot soldiers.

Morris dancers
at Aston-on-Clun

Nowhere does the countryside invade the town to better effect than in Craven Arms. 1,000 square metres of grass think they're a roof. The Shropshire Hills Discovery Centre has a grassy umbrella that supports over 70 tonnes of turf

Burwarton Show is "the best one day show in the country." The farmers club held their first show 110 years ago. Minsterley has the honour of Shropshire's oldest agricultural show. Nowadays it's held on a beautiful site in Lea Cross overlooked by the Stiperstones and bordered by the River Rea.

In Celtic times the shepherds decorated a prominent tree for their fertility rites. In Aston-on-Clun they celebrate Arbor Day, with tree-dressing, and a fête. A children's pageant remembers the 1786 wedding of a local squire.

Burwarton show

From parkland to cottage gardens at least a dozen are open under the National Gardens Scheme. Mouth-watering cakes await the visitor

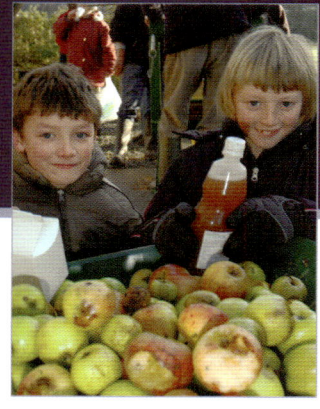

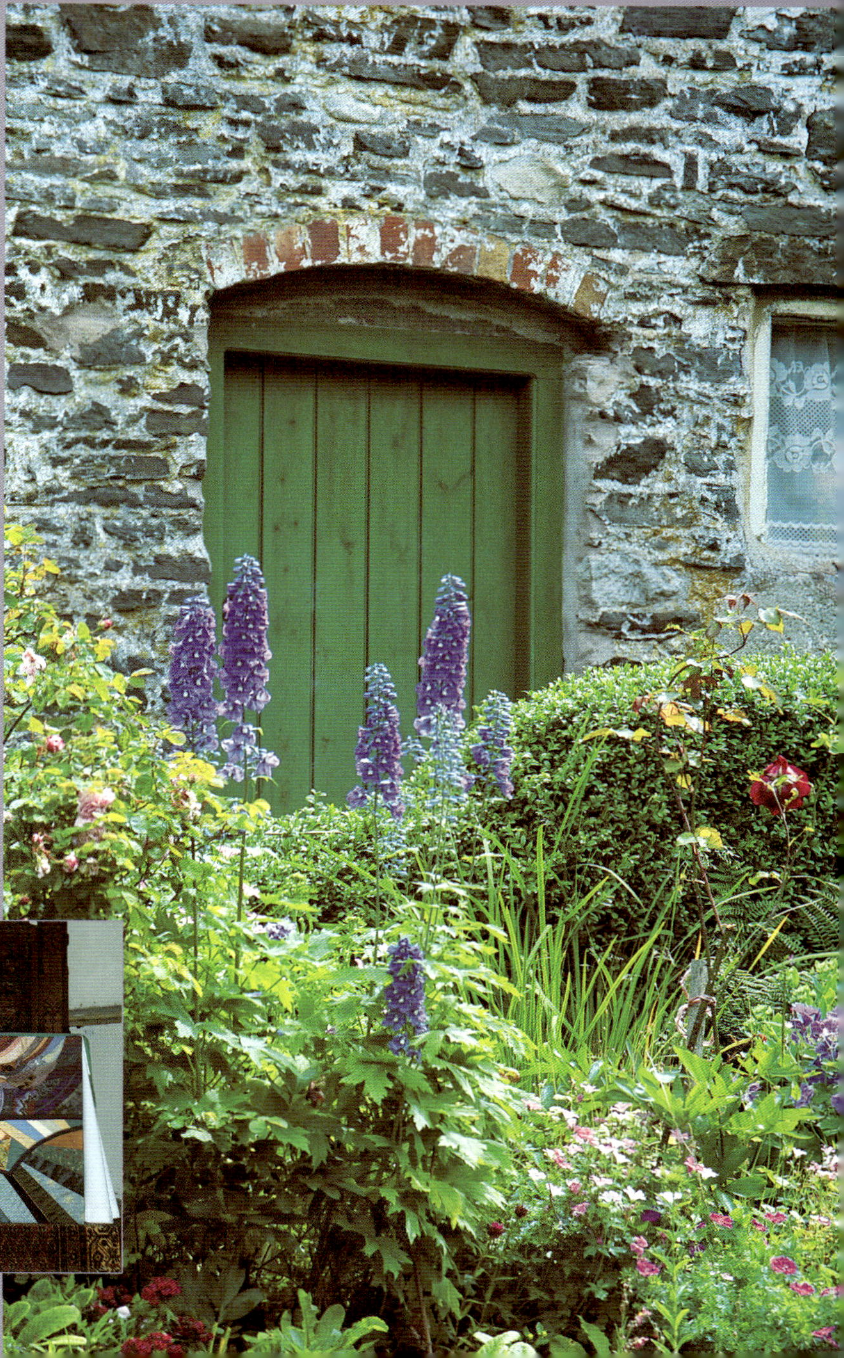

Don't miss Church Stretton's Apple Fair for proof of nature's amazing variety. The Acorn Restaurant dispenses the most imaginative apple-based dishes. Connoisseurs relish the cider bar and the competitive try to pip each other for the longest apple peel. Throughout the Shropshire Hills the hunt is on for 'lost' types of apple, whilst in tandem growers are encouraged to bring back decaying orchards to productive life.

"Wherever you are in the Shropshire Hills the chances are you are within easy reach of a parish churchyard. Of all the grassland in the hills the churchyards', alone, may have survived undisturbed for hundreds of years." Consistent with the need for respect for the dead, the wildlife and heritage, many churchyards are being conserved under the Caring for God's Acre project.

Quality craft work, Bishop's Castle

Shropshire Hills in an altar cloth, Bishop's Castle

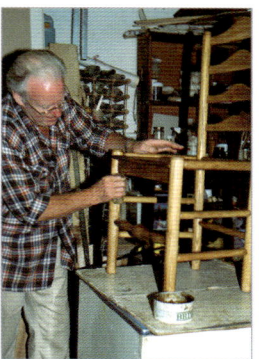

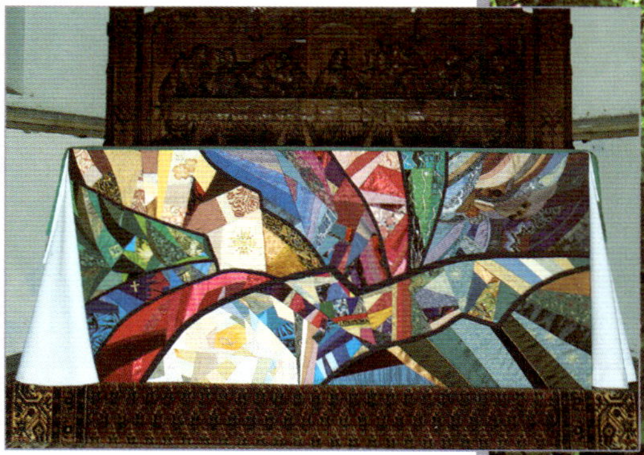

A millionaire couldn't buy these views and they're yours for free

Perkins Beach, Stiperstones

Hand-crafted in Shropshire

Do you prefer a solitary walk wrapped in thought or communing with nature? How about a jolly ramble with good friends? The glories of this landscape are not hard to find. There's no trudging for a couple of hours to find peace and quiet or a decent picnic spot. The best views and tranquillity are usually just minutes away.

Local shops and visitor outlets have walks books and leaflets for every area. Or visit the many websites. Walking for Health, ramblers, amblers and even shamblers will find a group to walk with. Whether you can tackle a hundred-mile hike, including all the major peaks, or are more likely to end up giving the kids piggybacks, the Shropshire Hills has something for every age and experience. Bishop's Castle and Church Stretton have annual walking festivals.

How about a guided walk to stretch your mind as well as your legs? Each year there is a walk for every season; from snowdrops in February to fungi in October. Early birds may like to be up with the Dawn Chorus. Rock fans can get more closely acquainted with Caer Caradoc, the Long Mynd or Wenlock Edge.

Don't allow our 'hills' to keep you out of the saddle. Where there are hills there are valleys. The green valleys of Teme, Clun and Redlake combine to offer "the most perfect cycle route we have ever found", according to one local specialist.

More challenging, the new National Cycle Route meanders over the border hills between Minsterley and Bishop's Castle. The effort is rewarded with spectacular views.

Routes from the Discovery Centre in Craven Arms range from "some hills but not too many" to "some very steep climbing and a steep ascent." New guides are being developed all the time. Rides from Bishop's Castle, Church Stretton, Cleobury Mortimer and Ludlow are next in line.

In the Forestry Commission's Hopton Wood, mountain bikers in search of thrills will find all the berms, descents, jumps and turns they could wish for. The site's 20 miles of forest roads and tracks include six miles for novices and young children.

Quiet countryside

Blue skies and blackthorn: early spring at Acton Scott

On Stapeley Hill

Near Inwood, Long Mynd

Bluebells, Hope Valley

You would expect the county that gave birth to the most successful jockey in racing history, Sir Gordon Richards, to have lots to offer the rider.

The Jack Mytton Way forms a spine for day rides and a long distance bridleway. From Much Wenlock to Llanfair Waterdine 45 miles of its length are through the heart of the Shropshire Hills.

There is a network of bridleways, byways and quiet lanes around the Long Mynd, the Stiperstones and Wenlock Edge. Ten circular routes from 10 to 16 miles have been compiled under the Ride UK project. Tireless work on foot and horseback has also identified the horse-friendly pubs.

'you float above the cares of the world.'

Walking above Clun

Floating over the Long Mynd

Traffic, Clee St Margaret

To appreciate fully the majesty and variety of the Shropshire Hills not even horseback is high enough. You need to soar. With the six-times British Hot Air Balloon Champion as your pilot "you float above the cares of the world."

Espiritu Balloon Flights specialise in flying over the Shropshire Hills with four launch sites in the AONB: Church Stretton, Linley Estates near Bishop's Castle, Plox Green and the Shropshire Hills Discovery Centre at Craven Arms.

If vertigo's a problem, then the Discovery Centre has the answer. For a simulated-but-oh-so-real ride over the Hills step into the basket of the hot air balloon. Magnificent aerial views without even leaving the ground.

The Shropshire Hills
Area of Outstanding Natural Beauty

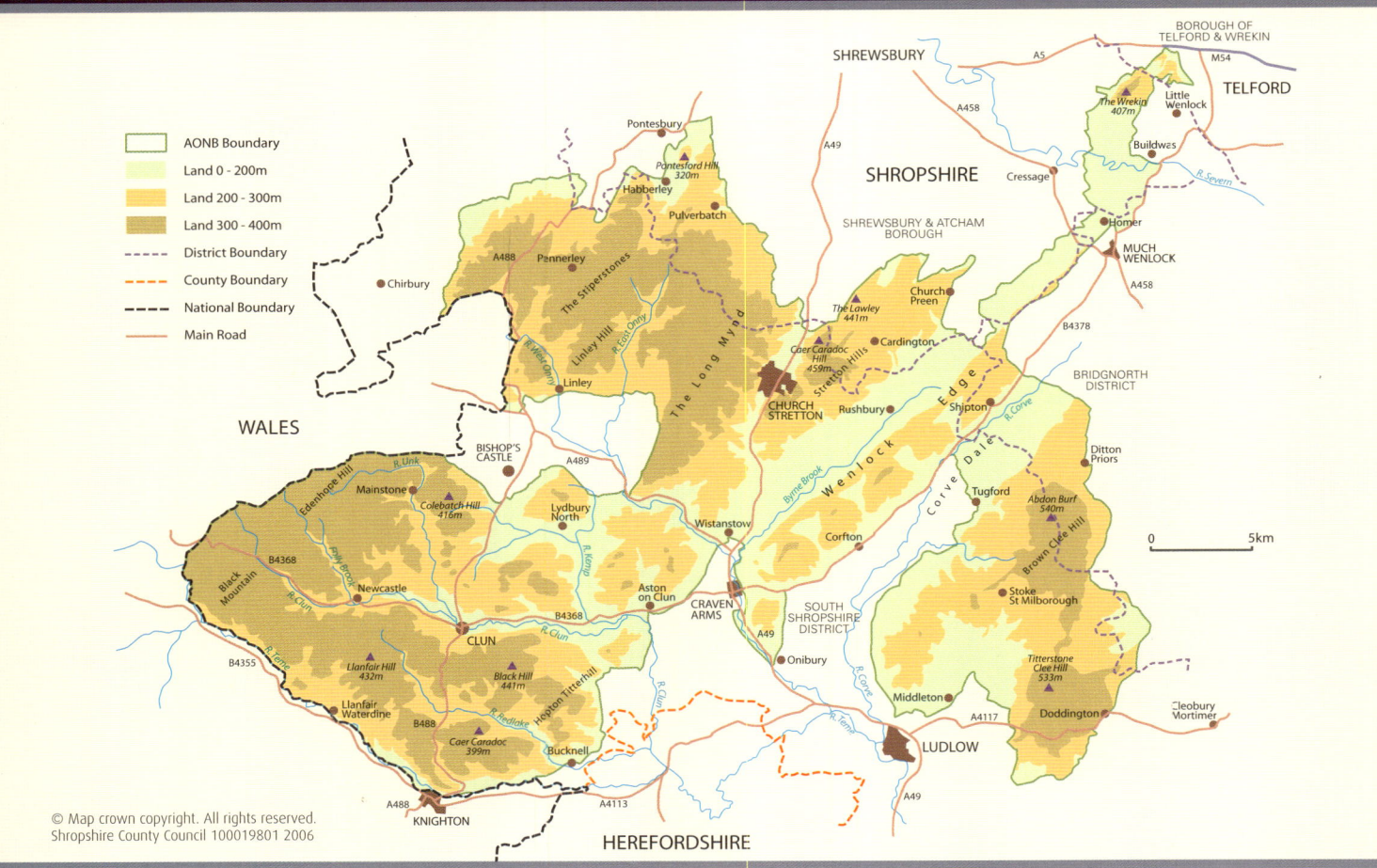

Legend:
- AONB Boundary
- Land 0 - 200m
- Land 200 - 300m
- Land 300 - 400m
- District Boundary
- County Boundary
- National Boundary
- Main Road

The AONB was designated in 1958 with the primary purpose of conserving and enhancing natural beauty. It is one of 41 AONBs in England and Wales. The AONB does not own or directly manage any land, but supports conservation through influencing policies for the area and by implementing projects in partnership. Five local authorities act jointly through the Shropshire Hills AONB Partnership. The Partnership has 38 members, the majority consisting of voluntary, private sector and community representatives.

The Blue Remembered Hills project increases community involvement in conservation through providing advice, grants and training. It focuses on particular features including veteran trees, wildflower meadows, riverside alders and orchards. Events, schools, volunteers and community groups are helped to implement landscape projects. The Heritage Lottery Fund has funded the project which runs from 2003 to 2007.

Shropshire Hills AONB Partnership The Old Post Office, Shrewsbury Road, Craven Arms SY7 9NZ
Telephone 01588 674080 Fax 01588 674099 www.shropshirehillsaonb.co.uk